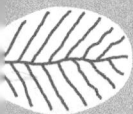

the earth
of you

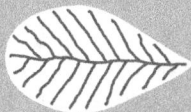

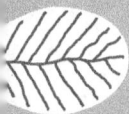

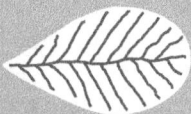

follow the journey of
'the earth of you' on instagram:

@fromrashi

for *you*,

you were, you are, and you always
will be close to my heart.

'you' refers to everyone who
has impacted my life even in the
slightest. good or bad. thank you,
because without you, i would
not be who i am today.

i wish to tell you how much it hurts.
but, most of all i wish to tell you that
it will only get worse from now on.

that you will feel so lost, you won't be
able to recognize yourself in the
mirror anymore.

that colors will start to look dull. that
sounds will drown your existence out.
that you will be so afraid of the power
you have in you to do something great
because you fear destruction is in your
very nature.

that you will isolate yourself until you
can erase every part of you that you
hate. that you will cross every limit
you set your heart out not to break
because you cannot distinguish right
from wrong, for they all look the same.
that you won't reach out to your loved
ones for help because you are ashamed
of feeling this way.

that the rain is no match for your
tears because you will cry and cry
until there is no more water in your
body to let go of.

then, you will break.

that you will spend days not thinking and not talking to anyone at all. minimal conversation.

that the quiet will become your new home. that you will learn with time everything fades. the sadness you felt will go away.

that after you are done feeling so sorry for yourself, you will pick yourself up broken piece by broken piece and take up your sweet time recreating the masterpiece of a puzzle you already were. that the emptiness will subside and you will feel whole again.

that you will open your eyes and observe how beautiful life really is.

that all you will have to do is get up out of your room and see the sun setting at 7:43 pm. that you were mistaken before because colors will start to become much more vibrant. that the sound of nature will always include you and make you feel complete.

and finally, you will admit it.

that you will not let yourself
justify what you did was right because
it wasn't. it was wrong, and you know
now to never do it again.

that you will fight past all of your
insecurities because you are now
strong enough to love who you are.
that you can do anything and
everything you will work hard for.

that feeling lost was the best thing
that could ever happen to you because
that is how you will find yourself in
the end.

but, i will not tell you any of this. you
will have to push your way through
and you will have to do it yourself.

be fierce. be kind.

be the love you know others do not
receive. be so loving all anguish
disappears.

this is how you will grow. this is how
you will heal.

rashi r. sanghavi

the earth of you

to love,
may i always see you the same.

you are reading
pages of my heart
pages of my soul
please do not rip them
if you do not agree

contents

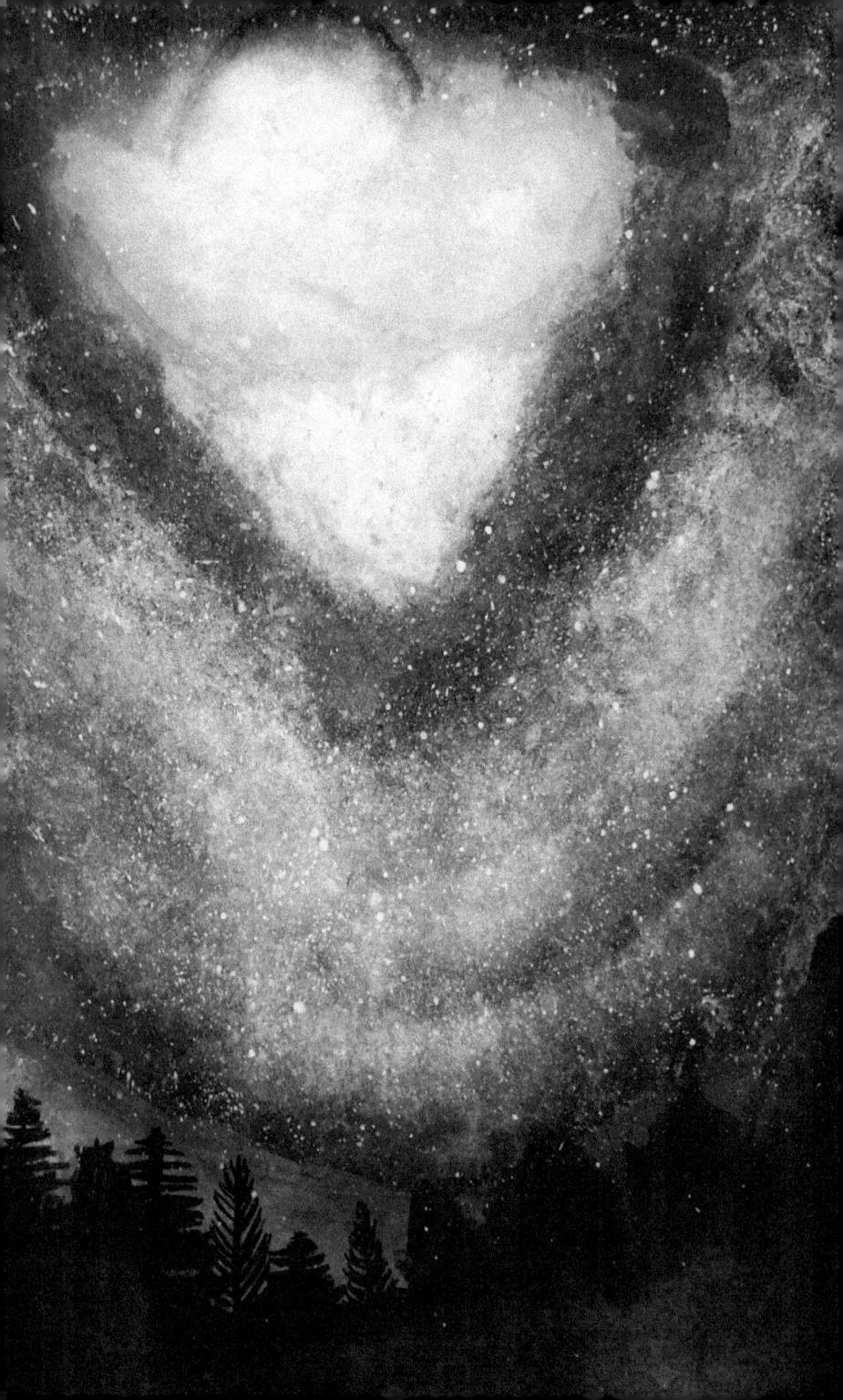

air

the earth of you

you asked me
to breathe for you

and i gave up the oxygen
i never had

—a fatal rescue

strong cannot ever feel weak
then what am i
when you are around

—*my weakness*

the earth of you

sometimes i wonder
if the air is filled with love
that is all you seem to
inhale and *exhale*

rashi r. sanghavi

no diving is permitted
when the waters
are shallow
but i still find myself
immersed
in a pool of you

—i will *dive* for you

i want to dance like
a ballerina
on the tip of my toes
reaching
spinning
grabbing
for the sky

—sky, *dance with me*

you gave me sleepless nights
so i decided to
wake you up in the morning

—good morning

we are
as wild
as leaves
when they
fall

—autumn, i miss you

souls connect
before eyes do
that is why
when my eyes first met you
i couldn't look away

—we are connected

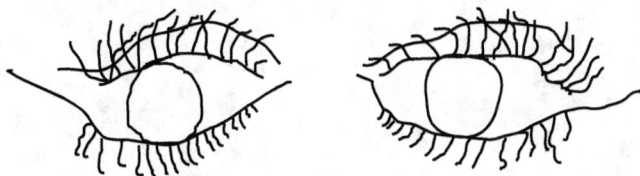

i dreamed of a place
where i wasn't *alone*
this place
welcomed conversation
longer than the night's dark
this place
illuminated your face with
a couple billion stars above

i dreamed of a place
where i felt truly *at home*
where my eyes
could meet your eyes
and grieve emotions
loud and strong and hard

—i dreamt a dream

they say you feel energized
around your soulmate
i will never forget how
it felt like awakening
from a lifelong slumber
as soon as my eyes
met yours
as if we could tell
just from one glance
we were meant to be

—when we met

why would i want
a love that is blind
i want a love
that is so beautiful
i could not take
my eyes off of it

—i am *mesmerized*

rashi r. sanghavi

within people i meet
there are stories
and i cannot help but wonder
if i will ever hear them

—*tell me more*

the earth of you

when you put my hands in yours
i pray that you feel warm
at home in the comfort of my fingers
so you never let go

when you tuck my hair behind my ears
with your big soft hands
i shake my head when you look away
so you do it again

when you look at me
i try not to blink
so you and i know the moment is real

when you come closer much closer
i feel your heartbeat pulsing on me
i breathe all of you in
so much better than oxygen

when you hug me
i wrap my hands all over your torso
and stand on the tip of my toes and
stumble back on purpose
so you catch me while i am falling

when you kiss me
i stop everything i am doing
and lean into your lips on me
so you know i feel the same way
about you as you do for me

—darling, *this is how you know*
you have fallen in love

my eternity
starts with *you*
and ends
with *us*

the earth of you

when i look at you
i fall into a trance
as if i am staring into
the city skyline
trying to memorize
every light that glows
every building that tries to stand up
just a little bit taller than the last
every crevice
that silhouettes the night sky
pretending that this
is the most beautiful sight
i have seen when really
it was always you

rashi r. sanghavi

i will hide from you
out in the open
so you will find me
always waiting to be found

—*hide and seek*

telling me the truth
and *only* the truth
is the best gift
you can give to me

—*what are we?*

rashi r. sanghavi

don't drive
your hands around me
why ride at roads
where you don't want to be

—*friends with benefits*

the earth of you

i know you

when something is up
you act a certain way
it does not stay unnoticed
not at all
not by me

—*i thought you should know*

if you can say
the same thing
calmly
why do you
shout at me

—i want peace

the earth of you

i will always give you
the option between her and me
what i believe is that
you should not be tied down to
anything or anyone
because in that lies suffocation
where something very special
dies a quiet painful death

i want to know that you will not
need to think who is better or worse
i want you to always pick me without doubt
but the second
you waver between us two
the second you forget
who loved you with everything to lose
and loved anyways....
do not pick me
pick her
i will know my love for you
was too much for you to handle
i will know that you thought i
was not good enough

—pick her

rashi r. sanghavi

no matter
which side you pick
you lose the other
as an option
will you
be able
to live with yourself
knowing that

—losing me

the earth of you

the door
will stay open
should you decide
to return

—second chances

rashi r. sanghavi

you give me
false hope
and i believe it
every day

my heart
speaks a language
you need not understand
if you are going to leave
anyway

—*foreign to me*

on days like these
i'll watch the blur around me
and feel as small as i possibly can
until i compress
the way my feelings already have

—feelings are too much work

i am willing to die for you
the sad part is
you would let me

rashi r. sanghavi

i'm feeling grey
in the middle
of black and white

seem to fray
at the edges
of wrong and right

—i am falling apart

the earth of you

it brings such sadness to pretend
not knowing the person
you knew better than yourself

—strangers *once more*

rashi r. sanghavi

i will say the same thing
over and over again in hope
that it will register
this time

—i don't believe

the earth of you

it's when the voices
around you get louder
that you lose yourself
completely

—out of mind

rashi r. sanghavi

pride
has always
gotten in the way
of my decisions

—pride, my predictable nature

the earth of you

something is missing
you can't seem to find what
feeling restlessly calm
and yet torn up within
you sound just a bit lost

—feeling lost

rashi r. sanghavi

rain will come and go
i don't want you to do the same

—stay with me

the earth of you

guide me
to believe
you will
never leave

—once is enough

rashi r. sanghavi

oh how easily you tell me to dream
and wake me up
before morning comes
dreams don't last
we don't last

the earth of you

don't ask obscure questions
you will end up with obscure answers

—i cannot explain

the strangers of yesterday
become dilemmas of this present day
stand ready
i predict a goodbye

the earth of you

fear filled my body
for just a second
my lungs closed
my veins delayed the blood
not running in my arteries
and i fainted
my left's and right's
confused with sways
every cell in my body burning
that is how i felt
when i lost myself

rashi r. sanghavi

if i didn't make
the same mistake twice
i would have been happy

—suffering

how many swipes
will take us to
our first hello

—online friends

rashi r. sanghavi

conversation
is only fun
when it works
both ways

—uninterest

the dial in my watch
never moves
it stopped working a while back
but i still wear it
for i want to remember
time was always frozen
when i was with you

—2:50 am

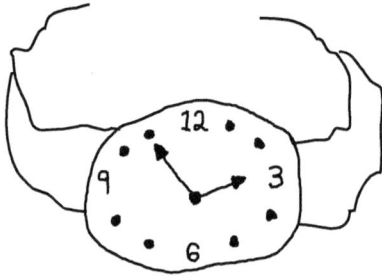

sleep child
pull those covers down
because one day
you will become friends with
the monsters underneath your bed

—scared at night

the earth of you

this is a broken record
that skips and stops
never continues to the next song
this is me
living
in my memories of you

—i cannot move on

rashi r. sanghavi

my memory of you has become so faint
all i have left of you is
the ground you walk on
and the air you breathe
i look for you everywhere i go

silly girl
don't be fooled
strangers who become lovers
were never friends to begin with

—lust

rashi r. sanghavi

what makes you inferior
is not forgiveness
but your incapability to ask for it

the earth of you

for me it is enough to see you alive
and breathing

—all i need

rashi r. sanghavi

make sadness your strength
and watch how everything falls into place
sadness isn't suffocating
it's empowering

the earth of you

standing and smiling
when i didn't want to
has never made me feel
this alone before

you are perfect he says
what he really means is
you are everything
he doesn't want to have

fire

the earth of you

it must be too early
i still flinch
to the sound of your name
every syllable
echoes memories
i shame

rashi r. sanghavi

can you look into
my eyes with your eyes
and tell me
they don't look empty

the earth of you

at the pit of my stomach
your name lies
echoing inside me
the form of longing
i could never rightfully
call mine

—you are not mine

rashi r. sanghavi

where there is hate there is love
hate cannot see love
so love hides behind me
until you catch her
in our little game of
hide and seek

—don't hate me

the earth of you

i am the high tides
that will drown you
if you come too close
so what makes you think
i will let you swim
when you try to leave

—don't leave

rashi r. sanghavi

did you ever
stop and think
maybe i should stay

—that maybe it's worth it

the earth of you

that *hello*
trapped
in your throat
was a devastating
goodbye

rashi r. sanghavi

when you remove people
from your life you don't
just stop talking to them
you take away their identities
as if they've never existed

the earth of you

i was a war
you did not want to fight

you gave me up
like a worthless casualty
in a battle i lost before
i could begin to survive

—some wars are left forgotten

rashi r. sanghavi

i want to come back and make
amends for everything
you said

i laughed as dry as i could
and i said
even the rain cannot wash away
all the stains of a broken heart

it will never be the same

the earth of you

do you
pull me back
because you know
i am trying to let go

rashi r. sanghavi

don't love a boy
more than you love sunsets
the sun will always
come back the next day
sadly he won't

—one night stands

the earth of you

you've already burned me alive
what makes you think
death fazes me

—i don't want to live

rashi r. sanghavi

my soul did not deserve wrath
whatever i did
to provoke you was not worth
twisting my soul into pieces

the earth of you

from which angle
did it look like
my love wasn't real

rashi r. sanghavi

have you seen sadness
when she wants to be happy
she doesn't smile she laughs
she doesn't shine she glows
she doesn't believe she knows
how empty she can be

—we all have masks

the earth of you

the voices inside my head
don't lie to me like you do

—you are a liar

rashi r. sanghavi

i think the most awful thing in the world
is sleeping with denim jeans on

the fabric is so tight on my skin
it reminds me of your warm embrace

the fabric is so rough
like your legs on top of mine

the fabric does not let me move
just like you when you are next to me

the fabric is so soft
it puts me to sleep

i was wrong
the clothes i sleep in that i hate the most
are nothing compared to your absence
right next to me when i wake

—i hate you more than i hate jeans

the earth of you

why are people pressurized
to move on after a break up
as if a train will leave you behind
a train people say
you must rush to catch
this should not be your standard of living
you have to live life
on your own accord
cry when you want to
breathe when nothing makes sense
eat bowls of ice cream at once
remember the good times and the bad
your life is not decided
at the will of train departures
tell those people
trains are old fashioned
we use ubers these days
they leave when we are ready
to move on with our lives

—we are modern

rashi r. sanghavi

i never knew why my mother said
take everything with a grain of salt
till you came around
and rubbed salt on wounds
life gave to me
and it clicked
everything hurts
just a little bit less

the earth of you

when i first met you
you looked like the sky
on the cloudiest of days

when i first touched you
you felt familiar like the cold rain
slipping through my warm hands

when you first left me
it was quiet
the kind of silence that is anything
but serene
before the storm
you left behind
raged on

—all heartbreakers come in three's

rashi r. sanghavi

a dangerous woman will say
mark my words
you are going to regret
not choosing me

the earth of you

i cannot do everything
perfectly
while standing
on the tip of my toes
your expectations
are way too high
for me to reach

—dear ma

rashi r. sanghavi

who are you to tell me how i can feel
how i can act
nag me
to fix my posture
tame my hair
look pretty at all times
only my insecurities are allowed to do that

—stay in your lane

the earth of you

i lost you
by your smile
when i stopped
making you happy

i lost you
by your eyes
when they stopped
getting lost in mine

i lost you
by your heart
when it no longer
beat for me

i lost you
when you made home
in someone else

—i can't find you

now i try so hard to separate
my heart
mind
and soul
as if being one again
would make me feel
the loss of you
all at once

—in pieces

the earth of you

you try
so hard to
keep alive
the flowers
that look best
while dead

—beauty is perception

rashi r. sanghavi

welcome to my funeral
i am a walking memorial
from the minute
i wake and realize
the pain hasn't ended yet

—the death of me

the earth of you

i will love you
till my lungs give out
only because you have convinced me
that i must hold my breath underwater
at all times
to stop you from leaving

rashi r. sanghavi

one lie
makes the most
truthful man
dishonest

—untruthful

the earth of you

every step i take back
four steps you take forward
my life isn't a board game
you can roll a dice for

rashi r. sanghavi

you didn't touch my heart
where compassion lain
you touched my neck
where my chest began
where was i when you laid
your hands upon me first

—the fault is mine

for you
it is better
to keep me on the side
than to lose me completely
because you are unsure
of how much longer
you will want
to *toy* with me

—you played me

rashi r. sanghavi

she is not the *one*
guys spend the rest of their lives with
she is the girl before that
she is the one they experiment with
to make sure everything goes smoothly
like strawberry jam on bread
for the girl they decide is worth keeping
until then every other girl is a test match
away from the *one*
so go find another girl
to screw with
mess with her heart
and her life
another conquest
one more notch on your bedpost
an innocent girl
who will believe everything you say
because she is just that naive
i am just another girl
i was just another girl

—the other girl

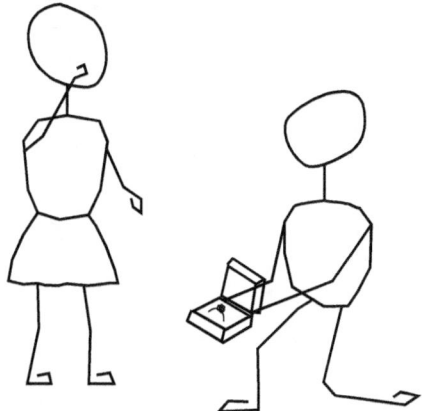

the earth of you

you cannot help people
who do not want to be helped
you may try to change lost causes
but i pray you do not forget
the results may be disappointing

that i loved you
or
that you didn't

—what hurt me more?

give me a boon
amnesia at my fingertips
to forget everything
highs and lows
make them go away
wanted and unwanted
give me a dying wish

rashi r. sanghavi

loving the ones
i held most dear
spun a hurricane
out of me

—when i shouldn't have

i have everything
to survive
but nothing
to live for
does that
sound familiar

—i have no meaning

rashi r. sanghavi

no stardust needed
when everything about a human body
is magical
i can touch
i can taste
i can see
i can hear
i can sense all of you
while you take it away from me

—you stole my magic

the earth of you

when you come across a mirror
do you shut your eyes
and shatter glass
like i do

—i broke my reflection

rashi r. sanghavi

men
women go to the bathroom together
where there is space to
gossip
put on makeup
openly act like girls
because wanting a little freedom
is too much to ask for

the earth of you

was it the rain
or our tears
that felt
so wet on my face
when you took me
outside in the storm

hugged me so tight
i could not remember
where your body began and mine ended
for two whole minutes so did you

and took yourself off of me
looked me in the eyes so hard
i blushed when you said goodbye
because it was the most beautiful way
someone
had ever left me before

—everyone leaves

rashi r. sanghavi

like pieces of a puzzle
my heart is scattered
amongst all the people
who have taken shards of me

the earth of you

black reminds me
that i will be
more empty
than i will be happy

rashi r. sanghavi

what

did i know
dyeing my heart black
to hide it from the darkness
would not spare me
from dying on the inside

no
i most certainly did not

—black hearted

the earth of you

my life is not in your hands
a bird will learn to fly
when it is meant to
as will i

rashi r. sanghavi

i will not fight
for what you
should already
want to have

—*me*

the earth of you

i said that
to hurt you
i wanted to show you
my capability to hurt you
was *no less* than yours

rashi r. sanghavi

we give advice to others
and refuse to listen to it ourselves
why is that so

—we are *hypocrites*

the earth of you

i found the soul in me
swimming in a lake nearby my house
i watched her start to get tired
arms droopy head swaying
she was going to drown
and i almost didn't save her
because i didn't want to be me

—save yourself before you can't

rashi r. sanghavi

you killed
the part of me
that wanted
to live

—this always happens

the earth of you

they crawl under your skin
and when the time is right
they bite
from layers deep down
they infect you with the seven sins

—toxic people are poisonous

rashi r. sanghavi

pain
can be
beautiful

—addict sometimes

the earth of you

your whispers
still sound in my ears
i told myself to remember your voice
next time i find
people like you
i can tell them
to never talk to me

—i want nothing to do with you

rashi r. sanghavi

i was told
i could never be the girl
i wanted to be
that some dreams
were not reserved for me
a story from an hour
i cried a sorrow sea

the earth of you

we promise that it's forever
we are talking sins
wait a little longer until you
or me do something wrong
forever becomes never
this is who we are

—commitment is not us

without you
breaking
my every hope
i couldn't have been
this strong

—thank you

you always say
situations change
and people shouldn't
then why is it so
you always leave
when they do

—you've changed

rashi r. sanghavi

eyes on the prize
you told yourself
when you wanted to
take the life out of me

—lifeless

the earth of you

every woman has two sides
do not force her to unleash
the one you fear most
and don't say i didn't warn you

—you've been warned

rashi r. sanghavi

they said my culture was lesser than theirs
they said my skin was too dark
therefore too ugly
i watched as the words left their mouths
and i said
my first culture is that of being human
my second culture is that of my parents
i am sorry that my name tag
does not match yours
my skin is the same tan
you long for in summer
so tell me
why is the beauty of my complexion
only relevant once a year

—self culture

the earth of you

you are the virus
i let into my body
willingly

—get out

rashi r. sanghavi

what's mine is mine
and it will never
be yours

—i am mine

the earth of you

goodbyes aren't unpleasant
the ones who give them are

—you are unpleasant

rashi r. sanghavi

i threw soil on your face
hoping you would grow
from your games

—grow up

the earth of you

devious they are
thoughts of course

they keep tricking me
to think of you
some irritablility
i have not yet surpassed

rashi r. sanghavi

the most
obvious things
are blind to me

i don't grab my keys
sitting on the kitchen counter
before leaving the house
or put my dirty socks
in the laundry
i just loaded for wash
or open my eyes and see
your real intentions for me
all you ever wanted
to do was play
and i was your game

the earth of you

expecations lead
to the death
of great things
shriveling them up
leaving no room
for them to grow
just like *you* and *me*

rashi r. sanghavi

did you think i wasn't enough
when your lips found someone else's
or when you said we would never work
that we were just too different
of people for us to find happiness
do tell how does a bee know
there is no more pollen left in a flower
to pollinate
without searching for it
you say the fault is in me
without seeing where you lack
oh honey
i am so enough
your two hands couldn't hold all of me
and say i was not enough
without it feeling satisfyingly
more than enough

—i wasn't enough

the earth of you

you mistake my kindness for weak
i am not rainbows and sunshine
for i am a storm
that ships do not dare sail through
you should hope
i never stop by your home
for i flood cities and towns with my rain
the sounds of lightning and thunder
are music to my ears
i help plants grow but know
i can make them drown if i wanted to

—i am strong

rashi r. sanghavi

you always gave
your love to me in alms
because i let you think
charity began at home

—beggars cannot be choosers

the earth of you

there are three types of people
in our world of heartbreak
strangers who become friends
you welcome with open arms
friends who become lovers
that never stay apart
and sadly
i see this way too often
lovers who become strangers
they drown people out of their lives
as if memories shared and cherished
never mattered
at all

rashi r. sanghavi

my mother and father
were superheroes
they used to soar through the sky
until they fell down and bruised
all just for me

—i am a villain

the earth of you

what is beast without beauty
they said you should know
you are one anyway
for a split second i was stunned
that looking the same as everyone
was the standard of beautiful
the next second
i gave them what they wanted
i showed them little hairs on my arms,
eyebrows unkempt
the third second
i saw disgust churning in their eyes
and i smiled with my not so perfect teeth
because confidence is beauty to me

—this beast is beautiful

ever since i was young
i have mistaken my thirst for hunger
always giving my body food
to quench a thirst
no land has the water for
leaving me even more confused why
my body never knew of satisfaction
no wonder why
i unrightfully believed
my want for you
was a need

—i don't need you

water

the earth of you

i was the ground
you walked on
until it grew a tree
and i rose from you

—i am above you

rashi r. sanghavi

you learn by day
that it doesn't hurt
as much as
it used to

—heartache

the earth of you

you love in grams
so careful of how much
of yourself you give away

—you don't want to get hurt

i will let you go
because i love you
and watch you walk miles on miles
away from me until the time is right
and stand right where i was when you left
so i can see you running back to me
out of mind out of breath
so ready to drink me in once more
and if you don't
i guess you and me
were never meant to be

—i love you, don't forget that

loving is losing
the idea love is lost
loving is loving even when
there is no one left to love

—love is love

rashi r. sanghavi

we always hold our breath
are we this afraid to let go

—*breathe*

the earth of you

i screamed i wish i wish
on the top of my lungs
on a little tiny mountain
far away from my house
where the echoes never come
but the wind takes it far
exactly to where you are
i was hoping
the wind would come around
with you in its arms
and deliver you in my hands
so i never let you go
because the last time that i did
i cried hell for years straight

—you are a part of me

rashi r. sanghavi

if i could rewrite the stars
our constellation would stay the same
i wouldn't change
a damn thing about you

—stay the way you are

the earth of you

one boy out of *billions*
broke your heart
tell me
is it fair
to blame all
for the actions of *one*

rashi r. sanghavi

our paths are very similar
but honey
we're miles apart
too bad our paths
never cross again

—perpendicular to me

the earth of you

the way the moon revolves
around our earth is not
the way i care about you
the way the moon blushes
a dirty pearl white
when it sees the sun is

—the way i care about you

love at first sight
no i don't want that
that is for people
who believe love is shallow
i want a love that stays
through the dirt of my tongue
pure as water
clean as salt
i want a love that pains
every damned second of the day
a love so timeless
there is no language it could hide
a love so warm
the sun runs dry
a love so wild
it catches my eye
the way moonlight serenades
my window at night
love is love is a love is a love

—pain, my love

the earth of you

they ask
why do i sleep so much
i say
so i can dream wonderful dreams
where i can learn every language
there is to speak
for when you say
i love you
je t'aime
mujhe tumse mohabbat hain
i will never
miss it again

—dreams are a wonderful place

rashi r. sanghavi

dear animosity
i haven't seen you in a while
don't be shocked
my soul banished you
you are not welcome here

—animosity stay away

the earth of you

i've always been
the glass is half empty
or half full kind of girl
but lately i'm the flow
that quenches your thirst
earthly and satisfying

—i am like water

rashi r. sanghavi

they say i'm really slow
but maybe
i just don't want to be fast

the earth of you

to reverse the effect of excess salt
do not add sugar
you have to add water

—*a subtle balance*

once the energy travels
through my hands to your hands
it will guide its way up your veins
and reach your heart
mending all broken lanes
to your lungs and your brain
what was an altered you
will become free of pain

the earth of you

i didn't grow my courage
to lose it in one shot
it's time to *try again*

rashi r. sanghavi

appreciate what you have
some things you cannot replace

—i miss you

the earth of you

thinking of you
feels like coming home
after a long day
soothing

if you were land and i was sea
i would move with the waves
and find myself in the space
between land and sea
where sand would hug me
the way your hands
would never let me go

the earth of you

beauty came from her home
in the cupboards of containers
stored with spices and turmeric mixed
with a few tablespoons of
milk applied to her face
her arms and her legs
before she got married
at eighteen years of age
a few years later beauty was raising
two kids by herself
while her husband was away
an ocean from it all
earning in the land of big opportunities
losing the sight of my
brother and i's childhood
she kept the word family together
clutched in her hands by the letter
beauty was in breaking
her home and building
a new one in new jersey
basically in the middle of nowhere
lastly beauty was in her
because she did all of this
when she was my age
all alone with my entire world
on her shoulders
for i could not do it
the same way

—thank you ma

rashi r. sanghavi

i mistook love for you
when it was really my dad
after every fight over
the littlest of things
today was about
not making him tea after
i made some for myself of course
i would strut up the stairs and
lock myself in my room
fifteen minutes later
he would yell
the entire house echoing the sounds
i love you
two seconds go by
i love you too

—i am daddy's girl

the earth of you

where in my mind will you live
when there is nothing left of me
to continue dreaming

—my imagination fails me

rashi r. sanghavi

no one likes
me for me
they just like
what they see

the earth of you

don't write me love letters
to define us on a sheet of paper
we are so out of this world
the words will not come alive
the way we do
when we touch
the words
simply do not exist

don't write me love letters
even though every part of me
wants to know
what you think of me and why
i need to know if there is
something that drives you
insane like when i let my hair
loose and it gets
wild in your face
or when i try to annoy you
and it doesn't work
so you play along and
let me believe i've won anyhow

don't write me love letters
to tell me i look cute
when i wrinkle my nose
your eyes already show me
immense adoration when i do
you have this spark in you
lips together eyes on me
looking as if i am the only reason

rashi r. sanghavi

you live to see every morning
after you bid me goodnight
nine hours prior to when we woke
hand in hand heart in heart
not wanting to untangle
because alone
you are missing from me

don't write me love letters
should the universe find out
you love me
it will take you away
until it believes you have forgotten
who i am to you
so i pretend i do not care
what you do and you say
for the universe should not know
i love you
more than it loves me

don't write me love letters
is what i will always say
secretly wishing that you do
for together you and i
can create our own language
with words made of us

—this is my love letter to you

the earth of you

i hope we still taste
of lemon and honey doused
in water years from now
so when we experiment with people
not meant for us
that leave us far more thirsty
than we began with
life draws us back together
because only you and i
can drink each other up

—we are satisfying

rashi r. sanghavi

you are alone yet
you do not feel lonely
that is called
self love

the earth of you

we live in a very *big* world
where people have decided to
divide and conquer
to make it very *small*

rashi r. sanghavi

we were the two wrongs
that could never make a right

—it wasn't destiny

the earth of you

i've been keeping up with this persona
of who i am really not
feeding my being with lies to hush it down
but these lies as my mother told me
were not good for my entity
it was only in due time
that they caught up with me
and now i feel all alone

—*is anyone there?*

rashi r. sanghavi

it is only when you
are alone
that the right people
will come
and show you
how much fun
it is to do nothing
together

—find them

always angry at the world
i neglected to see
how anger affected
the stubborn weight
my shoulders carried

—my back hurts

rashi r. sanghavi

you are the reason
i wish to accel
you are the reason
i live despite it all

—*bhai,* you never gave up on me

the earth of you

you handpicked me
from your mother's garden
i was the most full flower
you ever laid your eyes on
my petals were soft
and thorns ever wild

your mother told you
to love the flower whole
and it would bloom

so you took me everywhere
held me in your hands
laid me down next to you
said how much i meant
and i opened up for you

your eyes gleamed
and you smiled with a glow
you were truly happy
you had accomplished your goal
that day was our best

suddenly satisfied
and tired of the work
it takes to love something great
you stopped watering me
my brightness started fading
one by one my petals
wilted and the sight of me
became distasteful

rashi r. sanghavi

so you returned to the garden
the next morning
and picked the next
beautiful flower you could find
leaving me used and broken
from where you first saw me
saying this time
things will be different

if only you knew
we were different
all you had to do
was let me love you
without break
until you realized

dead flowers
can look better
than the ones alive

—use and throw

the earth of you

there is music in silence
you dance my way
when i give it to you

—waltz with me

rashi r. sanghavi

my darling
you will roar
even outside
the cages
that try to
keep you in

the earth of you

your shadow has never
left your side
whether or not you decided
to give it the light of day
that is how you will find me
always ready to listen
anywhere anytime

—i am listening

rashi r. sanghavi

not every text
deserves a reply
and not every reply
deserves
to be left on read

—first world problems

i love you
means shit
if your actions
do not account
for your words

—i love you

rashi r. sanghavi

your moonlight serenade
made the stars shine brighter
the sky feel darker
and the moon glow whiter
your silence grew at my love for you
and then you fled
leaving me to sing
my own
stardust blues

that okay
is not okay
and it never will be
just an okay
okay?

rashi r. sanghavi

it was the first time
i saw you in months
and i saw your vulnerable eyes
piercing mine
attempting to unlove
whatever you had seen in me
while i gave you a broken smile

—is this real?

the earth of you

i wish i stopped looking
for success in all the wrong places
before i scarred myself into believing
i was good for nothing
this mistake formed a hole in me
that grew bigger and bigger
until my lungs collapsed
and i no longer spoke
that i could do anything
because i believed
success was always necessary

—let the hole heal

rashi r. sanghavi

i will show you around
a vast sea of blue
i shed my tears in

—let's go boating

the earth of you

those eyes you were given
were meant to sail oceans not tears

rashi r. sanghavi

how do i pretend
not to love you
without hurting you

the earth of you

you loved me
the way you watered your plants
so determined
for each bud to bloom
you were a natural
until one day
you drifted away from the thorns
further from the petals
and they wilted and died
i guess you willfully
'forgot' to water them for a year

—i need watering

rashi r. sanghavi

if i do not say upfront
then i want to be vague
i want to be so ambiguous
it would take you days
to figure me out

the earth of you

my mother has lived her entire life
in four walls and a small kitchen
and dear me you have no idea
how she ruled it like a queen
i was told my body is a palace
whose walls i must adorn
with silver and gold given by my mother
from her mother's mother
for the man who would live inside
these generations have taught me
tradition must continue on
even if the weight of silver and gold
crushes me whole
the leftover scars will start stories
to tell the next generation
that it is possible to survive
amidst silence that burns all words
into ash little do they know
i want to thrive, day in day out
speak my mind without worry
whom it may concern
start a life where my ma is proud
for living in a world much different
than hers
where palaces are adorned
with personality and knowledge
not my life dangling onto doors
made of gold

—palaces don't need silver and gold

rashi r. sanghavi

a lotus
sprouts in murky water
blooming pink and white
not always perfect but
always beautiful
why aren't we this confident

—insecurities

the earth of you

be careful what you wish for
your wishes do
set foot into this universe
sometimes they find
their way back to you
whether you like it or not
what you wish
may come true
what you wish
might not help you

rashi r. sanghavi

before you paint
your arms with knives
ask yourself
is the agony worth it

—self harm

the earth of you

to move
to think
to feel
it hurts

i haven't felt
this kind of pain
since you left

rashi r. sanghavi

my heart
poured
said
and
unsaid
into my lefty hands
and so i wrote

being feminine
is a cause
not a reason
i should have
to give to you

rashi r. sanghavi

courage walked through the door
all ready to associate itself with me

—feeling whole again

the earth of you

people have thought you
to be this person
prove them wrong
because
you know
that person
is not you at all
with naturalness
your kind nature
will turn
their judgemental eyes
into ones filled with love

rashi r. sanghavi

with good heart
and determination
my dear
you are invincible

the earth of you

become my moonlight first
before you dream to be my sunshine
stay the night
through my darkest despairs
comfort me
tell me it is okay
not to be okay
tell me that the long night
will become a beautiful sunrise
one will just have to stay up to see it
then i will say
i saw you then
and i see you now
you are my sun
you are my moon
you are my entire universe

—moon and sun

rashi r. sanghavi

you are my sunset
let me watch you

the earth of you

i fell in love with you
completely
wholly
and that was the problem

there was none of me left to share
with you i had no personality
i became the girl
who was so dependent
for acceptance and love

you must have felt suffocated
and for that i am sorry

rashi r. sanghavi

i was too busy chasing others
that i did not realize
you kept my rainbows alive

and when you left
the colors did too

—a colorless world

the earth of you

we leaned on each other so much
i forgot what personal space was

—no space inbetween

rashi r. sanghavi

shrewd candles
they always know
the mood it puts us in

—divine scents and glow

the earth of you

people put on a mask
to hide their emotions
as do you
you think you are
dramatic and burdensome
but no
you are not insufferable
you are magnificent
your story is worth to be told
to the entire world
so when i offer
to put a leash on your mask
and pull it far
far away from you
do not see me as a mad man
going on and on about
something that does not matter
you lie to yourself
by saying you do not care
about this emptiness you feel
because you fail to see
this feeling does not go away easily
and when that person
is willing to help you
take their help
they will share what has helped them
and now
you will share what has helped you

—share your emptiness

rashi r. sanghavi

people are like mountains
once you get to know them
you start climbing their steep terrains
some shorter than others
and some longer than others
at the top you look back and see
how far you have come
you realize it has been a rocky road
on your way up
the path is even worse
on your way down
you stumble and fall
this time bruise too
best to stand exactly where you are
stay exactly where you need to be

—we all climb

the earth of you

love was by my side
and the sky ripped it apart
love energized my being
and the ocean drank every bit
love was all warm and sun
and the night stripped color away
love sang to me midnight blues
and the earth ate its voice
love lit me a candle
and the wind blew it out
love fought the world so hard
because the world knew
i didn't appreciate love at all

—when love fought for me

rashi r. sanghavi

please understand two things about me
i will never
stop you from going
but i will never
let you go from my heart

earth

oh darling
you were woven
with warmth in your fingers
love in your soul
and rigidity in your bones
don't let them break you

—fear no one

rashi r. sanghavi

i cannot afford
to be dead
from the inside out anymore
the times where i would stay awake all night
looking at my ceiling in the dark
for answers i could not find
are gone

the earth of you

when i ask you about your body
i never want to belittle you
i thought a creation so beautiful
it was open for discussion

—to all the girls out there

rashi r. sanghavi

you are not here
still my mind is on you
i cannot let you go
you are everywhere

the earth of you

it is of necessity
people come and go
and it will break your heart
when they leave
welcome you must say
and greet them as they leave
give them reason to return

rashi r. sanghavi

i am expanding on my horizons
i believed you were the sun
who would set in my evenings
i was wrong to think it was never me
who would rise every morning
when you would leave me

—i rise

the earth of you

lots of love
will come to you
when you
stop expecting
it to come

—when you're expecting

rashi r. sanghavi

you think you don't fit in
in this big spacious world
only because they
did not give you
the room to breathe

—you do fit in

the earth of you

i let you consume me
because i was empty

—i used you for me

rashi r. sanghavi

i know the way you feel
doesn't scare you
as much as letting go
of that feeling does
it's that shoulder
you can always cry on
and because of that
you let it consume you

the earth of you

heaven and hell in the same day
is what you gave me
the best part is
i don't know
which of the two ended worse

rashi r. sanghavi

there was a time not too long ago
before the hurting
i used to smile at the clouds
and dance with the birds
where is she
i miss her

—she grew up

the earth of you

the skies are moving
and color is emotion
skies fill with orange and pink
and purple and black
none of this means anything
unless you set the sun yourself

—setting the sun

rashi r. sanghavi

see
this hiccup
did cure

—i told you so

the earth of you

if i am the first one to feel this way
bless my words
to make you feel
that tremble
ache in your bones

rashi r. sanghavi

i rise in the east
i fall in the west
if anything but the sun
i am human before all

we rise and we fall
the difference is
how fast
we are willing to get up

the earth of you

because people have failed you
you will not fail them

sail oceans for the people who refuse
to cross puddles for you
remember
you reap what you sow

—what goes around comes around

rashi r. sanghavi

to cleanse myself of negativity,

i like to drink warm water mixed
with 2 tablespoons of lemon
the warm water burns unkind words
still trapped in my throat;
the first tablespoon of lemon
soothes the ache my soul feels,
it endured so much wrath
so much grief and so much pain;
the second tablespoon of lemon detoxes
animosity and pride,
from my body to my aura — until i
lose myself again

—a natural cleanse

balance, it's a two way street:
breathe in breathe out

rashi r. sanghavi

my hands are out in front
of me facing upright
i accept positivity that
enters through my palms
and i expel the negativity that
lingers through my fingers

the earth of you

i do not have the heart in me to see you cry
lies
cry it out and put yourself together
in this world
you help yourself

—self help

rashi r. sanghavi

don't think
whoever you are
i want to conquer your love
before i find the seven wonders of my world

—it's not you, it's me

the earth of you

the amount of love you can give to others
is insurmountable
i promise your capability to love will never
fail you
a dose of love is all people need
to know that you are genuine

rashi r. sanghavi

maybe one day
the universe will give back to me
what i have given it

—the circle of life

knowledge is power
and when you don't want it
know that other people will take it

—choose wisely

rashi r. sanghavi

you weren't the first to leave
and so i won't cry

—all good things must end

you were the sun and
i was the moon
we never had the stars
written in our favor
so close
yet so terribly far

—distance

rashi r. sanghavi

as i feel unimportant
life reaches out to me
grabs me by the ear
and shows me that it cares

—life is my friend

the earth of you

we are fractions old
challenging a greater cause
for not loving us enough

—this universe

rashi r. sanghavi

i think we live in ancient history
and the stars are the books
we never chose to read fully

—skipping lines

the earth of you

i have no doubt
the big houses
and expensive cars
and lavish parties
look like dreams worth living
but i will dream
to live a simple life once more
where every little joy is my entire world
where there is no hate just understanding
where there is no excess money
but immense peace
where there is no bed but my mother's feet
that is a slumber
no one gives the luxury of having

it is so difficult to be simple
when everyone around you wants to be great
there is no greatness higher than simplicity

if there were
why do you always come around
to the things that are less complicated

—we are simple

9:00 am the alarm rings
you will
never be given
a reason to love
9:05 wake up
you just
do it anyways
9:07
even if
he won't
9:08
even if
he never did
9:10
love will always
brim over the edges
of your grief
and find you
the happiness
you never believed
you could have
9:14 stop staring
at him next to you
and wake him up

—love anyways

the earth of you

if thoughts make hearts beat
you make my pulse bleed

rashi r. sanghavi

the first offense is to push
everyone who cares away
the second offense is to
think you are alone

the earth of you

too many things running
in my mind made me
run away from me

—far from finish lines

rashi r. sanghavi

adorn
a string of pearls
on your neck
because you
want to be loved
by you

—self love

the earth of you

i love being here
breathing
earthing
every damned day
feels like walking
on holy land

rashi r. sanghavi

to be real it must be written
there must be a picture if it happened

—twenty-first century

the earth of you

our time
on this planet
is meant to help others
maybe we are broken butterflies
that have disastrous effects
had we been gone

rashi r. sanghavi

until the person of cause
does not realize he or she
is adding to your unending pain
please child
refuse suffering
you will know when it is worth it

—it is your pain to use

the earth of you

if it is meant to be
it will happen

—destiny

rashi r. sanghavi

when i stopped trying to fit in
in the places i did not belong
i found out
there was no puzzle left for me to solve

—i solved it

the earth of you

love and real love
are not the same thing
nor is there a thin line
separating the two
they are not
bordering countries
they are oceans
away from each other
oh honey
the love you are getting
is not the love you deserve
you are so much more
than the fake love
you call home
real love is constant
the kind that never changes
real love does not react
when you don't meet it's expectations
real love is a lifestyle
not some unwanted commitment
you are worthy of this

—i real love you

rashi r. sanghavi

say what you think
and mean what you say
be bold
no such thing as provocative
only then
has your mama
raised you right

—i am bold

the earth of you

i stopped letting myself live
because
somehow
someplace
something
was always
going to go wrong
it ate at me
licked
its
fingers
cleared
its
throat
then i destroyed the plate

—don't let worry eat away

rashi r. sanghavi

how long will we pretend
we never knew our souls
were meant to be together

—to the very end

the earth of you

distance yourself
from everyone, the ones
the ones that love you
will never let you walk away

rashi r. sanghavi

when you cross the line
and break values
you stood ground for
and sin day and night
i will shake the earth
as my response

—i value your values

the earth of you

for everything that hurts
treat it like a wound
be cautious and let it heal
some scab
some scar
some bloom

—the nature of healing

rashi r. sanghavi

failing because you aren't good enough
is not good enough
work at your goals till you meet them
it will take your blood sweat and tears
but realize when you need to stop looking
for success in the wrong places
before you hurt yourself even more

the earth of you

the earth of you
means
i will pull you back
to your roots
where you can let go of
whatever died inside you
and grow
wonderfully

this is not an end.
this is a new beginning.

afterword

i humbly thank you for reading to the
very end of *the earth of you.*

it has been four very long years that i
have nurtured these words into what
they are today. it was when i was just
fourteen years old that in my heart i
knew one day i would write my own
book. and i wrote it. i finally wrote it.

as a little girl, i wanted to help
people. naturally, becoming a doctor
seemed like a viable option as doctors
help people of all kind. this was all
that mattered to me (well until i took
advanced placement chemistry in high
school and failed miserably). my head
was telling me to keep going, but my
heart strayed away from this
dilemma. overall, i decided this was
not the right path for me.

i developed my knack for poetry in
middle school. ever since, poetry is a
way for me to speak without speaking.
as i started posting more and more
poetry on my instagram, @fromrashi,

i realized that there were countless
others connecting with what i wrote.
and somehow, someway, these words
helped people heal and grow.

it's quite amusing. the universe
showed me right from wrong, yet it
still listened to my childhood wish.

this book is for the people who need
to be grounded back to their roots.
the earth of you was written to show
you that you are allowed to feel every
emotion that comes your way as
ignoring such feelings will only hinder
your healing.

with this new year, i hope this new
beginning helps you grow to heights
you thought were unimaginable.

once again, thank you for being a part
of this beautiful journey.

rashi r. sanghavi

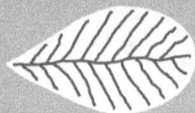

i know you were hurt
by everyone that has ever left
but people in your life
they enter for a reason
and they leave for one too
oh darling
it is okay
cry it out
mourn and grieve
and start anew
when they do
beginning with
the earth of you

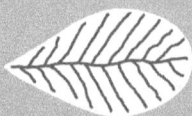

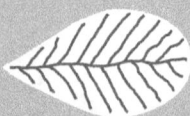

www.ingramcontent.com/pod-product-compliance
Lightning Source LLC
LaVergne TN
LVHW051358080426
835508LV00022B/2888